DELIVERANCE
THROUGH THE
WINDOW OF MY
MIND

DELIVERANCE

THROUGH THE

WINDOW OF MY

MIND

BRIAN E. DIXON

DELIVERANCE THROUGH THE WINDOW OF MY MIND

iUniverse books may be ordered through booksellers or by contacting:

iUniverse
1663 Liberty Drive
Bloomington, IN 47403
www.iuniverse.com
844-349-9409

Because of the dynamic nature of the Internet, any web addresses or links contained in this book may have changed since publication and may no longer be valid. The views expressed in this work are solely those of the author and do not necessarily reflect the views of the publisher, and the publisher hereby disclaims any responsibility for them.

Any people depicted in stock imagery provided by Getty Images are models, and such images are being used for illustrative purposes only. Certain stock imagery © Getty Images.

ISBN: 978-1-6632-5699-7 (sc)
ISBN: 978-1-6632-5226-5 (e)

Library of Congress Control Number: 2023948115

Print information available on the last page.

iUniverse rev. date: 05/07/2024

This book is dedicated to Chris Blackwell, Darren Dickison, and all others taken by the disease. In memory of Brent Joseph Dixon, who was murdered by people with this disease.

CONTENTS

ACKNOWLEDGMENTS

Special thanks to this list of perfectly imperfect people whom I consider superheroes:

Penney Medici Carlsen
Earl Carlsen
Chad Carlsen (Dr. Strange)
Kelly Carsen (Ice Queen)
Frank Buffa (Superman)
Ozzie (Superwoman)
Amanda Childs (Batgirl)
Eric, my counselor (Angel)
Peter Hernandez (the Rock)
Cindy Williams (Good Witch)
Elise Graves (Storm)
Bailey (Snow White)
Brittnay, the young blonde counselor (Innocense)
Tom (Underdog)
Christian Shelby (Captain America)
Ross Meniken (the Hulk)
Thomas O'Sullivan (Grandpa Incredible)
Brook Lazaro (Wonder Woman)
Cliff Puett (Fierce Competitor)
Johnny De La Cruz (Spider-Man)
George (the Gentle Giant)
Jonathan Barnard (Georgy Porgy)
Clint Servoss (Stretch)

Leslie (Phoenix)
James Wardrop (Ant-Man)
Andrew Marquez (Flash)
André Marquez (Flash's brother)
Zach in admissions (Captain Marvel)
Richard Holsinger (the Black Panther)
Greer Mitro (She-Hulk)

ONE

BORN INTO THIS TRIBE

was born on June 15, 1961, at 6:15 in the evening at Queen of the World Hospital on Thirty-First and Linwood, off Prospect, in Kansas City, Missouri. For years, I didn't find any significance in the time; only the date had any importance to me. I now believe that timed moments can have specific meanings, despite our lack of conscious awareness, in some particular moments in life. On the Chinese sign chart, the symbol of the rooster is in my hour chart. We all know the characteristics of the rooster, and now I proclaim a rooster's intent for those who still sleep in any form of addiction. I awoke to the realization of the cancerous effects that cause self-destruction of the spiritual and physical realms in my existence. Drugs and alcohol aren't the only strongholds hindering me from being a bright force and source in the spaces, places, and atmospheres where my physical and spiritual entities collide. I truly believe the portion of myself that I can't see but know exists was here long before my physical date in this dimension, and I feel it will exist for eternity through the forms of hosts.

I was born to Joyce Gail Clemons Dixon and Carl Frazier Dixon. My mother's mother was Lorraine Thomas Clemons, and she eventually married her second husband, John Brewer, who became my grandfather despite blood. My mother's father's name was

Raymond Clemons. He was my blood grandfather, and I remember him telling me some important advice. He told me, "Never let the next man work harder than you do, and, boy, pay yourself." I didn't understand what he meant when he told me, but it is to me now like a freshly painted picture. My father's mother's name was Luda Ray Dixon Miller, and her husband's name was Joe Miller.

My father didn't tell us much about his father for some reason, which I can only attribute to a lack of fatherhood. My father didn't introduce us to many of his relatives, and after learning bits of his story later in life, I used the art of reasonable deduction as I began to understand life and relationships. My father's mother was a businesswoman in real estate, and she eventually acquired several houses and buildings. My grandmother turned one building into a nightclub, pool hall, and restaurant on Fifth Street, between Quindaro and Parallel, in Kansas City, Kansas.

When I became of age, my father told me about and showed me the house in which he had been raised. In his first twelve years of life, he and his mother stayed with my grandmother Luda Ray's parents in a house on Third and Walker in Kansas City, Kansas. In my father's teenage years, he stayed with his grandparents while his mother ventured out to secure a firm financial status for her entire family. To her credit and my amazement, she eventually purchased a building on the plaza. I still struggle to visualize my grandmother as a madam who used several houses as brothels, gambling houses, and bootleg spots all in one.

At that centrally located business, my father met his future mother-in-law, who was an employee there. I was informed by other relatives that my father was also a sort of henchman, as he was one of the collectors for the gambling debts owed to my grandmother, his mother. The story was told that people would cross the street if they found themselves walking on the same side as my father, because if they owed money, he was known to have a one-hitter-quitter night-night punch as a collector. I never would have imagined this about my father or his family; however, small memories lend credence to the stories told.

My father's mother's house had an elevator, and on the third floor, when the doors opened one day, there were beautiful ladies dressed in servant or maid clothing, waiting to serve me as I entered the room. On another occasion shortly after that encounter, I was to be dropped off with my sister Kim at our grandmother's house, which was a different house. It had no elevator, but the same kind of dressed maids were ready to serve at the word of my grandmother. Some of these encounters helped me to piece together a portion of my past, which helped to make me who I am today.

My mother's mother, Lorraine Thomas Brewer, had the greatest impact on my life that I can remember. She and the people around her, kinfolk and friends, set the atmosphere and created the environment for who I am today.

I'll start with John Brewer, my grandmother's husband, who was not my blood grandfather but practically was closer to me than my grandfather Raymond Clemons. John Brewer was one of the coolest, most soft-spoken men in my past. He was in no way perfect, because he could tie one on with the best of them. He talked people out of their money with a smooth poker face while gambling, which could take him away from Friday night until Sunday morning. He would sometimes arrive with gifts and groceries, and there were times when he just showed up. My grandmother, after having an eventful weekend of drink, would be pissed off as she waited for his return.

One time, he called to check on her, and I remember the liquor in her voice as she threatened to whoop his ass when he got home. I was laughing on the inside, until she repeated, "Me and my grandson are going to whoop your ass."

I immediately began waving my hands in the background, as if my grandfather could see me saying, "No, no, not me," as I entered a bizarre state of anxiety as I too awaited his anticipated arrival.

My grandfather was a World War II navy vet who was in excellent shape. He and his friends would sit around the table, arm wrestling, and I watched him win repeatedly against all rivals. I would look at his muscles flex to a form I admired, and I remember him saying on occasion, "Man, I got muscles I ain't even used before," as I witnessed the arms of his opponents go horizontal.

My grandfather and grandmother had a few friends I'll describe with a few words that best recapture a depiction of my fondness I still hold dearly in my heart until this day: would-not-wear-deodorant Leroy; loudmouth Trigger and his wife, weed-smoking Mildred; Strong Man Bill; Cut-a-Man Duck; Georgy Porgy Emmitt; Walter, who was blind but could see what he wanted to see; Uncle Nemo, who said, "I love you, baby," while giving a nickel; Little Bill, who always said, "I can drink more than you," and his go-along-to-get-along wife, Merriam; poker-faced Uncle Robert and his don't-start-no-shit wife, Aunt Bert; Uncle Arthur, whose attitude was "You can't make me not smile," and his beautiful wife, Phyliss; willing-to-start-some-shit Aunt Ethel; Uncle Fred, who said, "You may or may not see me"; Aunt Bert's friend Phyllis, who said, "Boy, I'm gonna give you some when you grow up"; Auntie Rain, my mother's only sister, and her first husband, cooler-than-ice Uncle Richard; and Auntie Rain's second husband, Uncle Darrel, who made everybody laugh.

These individuals were a great part of my upbringing. We often got together, but the holidays in particular gave me deep sentiment with these characters placed center stage in the production of my life. I was at my grandmother's house, a seven-hundred-square-foot house, on many occasions with these people. The cozy house had a bedroom and bathroom combined, approximately 225 square feet. Toward the front were the combined kitchen and dining room, with a round table. That room was 250 square feet. That was where the magical cooking took place and where some of the most intimate conversations of enlightenment transpired for me in my adolescent and teen experiences. In the front was the living room, which completed the cozy little house. It was equal in size but carried the most impression. The living room hosted the description of love, which I covet till this day.

As described, the cozy house was small, and the people I mentioned, along with a few others, would gather on many occasions and most holidays. I now need to give more concise details about people I didn't mention in that small but cozy house. My oldest brother in Carl and Joyce Dixon's family was Darren, and my description, or term of endearment, for him was a karate master who just wanted to kick somebody's ass. My sister Kim's trademark was saying, "You missed me," while someone was swinging at her. My little brother Brent said, "I'll go Tasmanian devil if you push me too far." A few years later came our little brother Brad, whose trademark was "Here—hold this, dodo," and our first cousin Sherita, who said, "Take your turn being my best friend, or I'll turn on you in a minute." Sherita was the daughter of Auntie Rain, my mother's only sister. I'd consider myself biased if I didn't give a description of myself that everyone would agree upon, and that would be the following: curious-while-tearing-the-skin-off-anybody's-goat Brian. Or they'd say, "Better hide your toys from destroyer Brian."

I remember the smell and taste of Christmas as we, the kids in the family, found the short route to and from the small bedroom through the side door to the left of the bedroom.

The side door had a small porch with three steps that led us to the backyard, where a swing with two seats awaited our imaginative prowess on that particularly festive day. We brought out some of the toys gifted for Christmas as we traveled to and fro, in and out of the small bedroom. We learned where our spot was as children. Occasionally, grown-ups in need of the bathroom would pass through, holding a conversation with someone somewhere in the cozy little house. Often, there was laughter from some form of verbal banter occurring that a few were, or everyone was, part of.

The house was crowded, with six children or more in the bedroom. One used the chair, while the rest would secure spots on and around the bed. The dining room had a table with six chairs but room for only four to be placed around it. The front room had two recliners and a couch, and one of the chairs from the dining room table would be used. There were three or four folding chairs strategically placed to avoid impediment in the narrow pathways of the house. There were people who had no seat, who would stand until sitting spots appeared. The people standing often were asked to give way as people wanted to get close to someone else or pass by them to get a comfortable standing spot to avoid the narrow pathways. There was a large grate on the floor in the dining room, through which heat entered the house. Everyone looked forward to standing on it in the cold weather of the season.

There could be, at times, twenty-six people closely packed in the small, cozy house, and we would rub love on and toward one another as we maneuvered throughout the narrow pathways of my grandmother's little house. People were loud, people were laughing, people were drunk or tipsy, people were playing cards, people were listening to music, people were dancing, and they would allow the kids to come dance. The conversations would turn to the new dances of the next generation.

That was a time in my life when I felt loved and secure from the darkness that swirled in the world. I had no fear of what was to come, because I was entrenched in the moments of our lives as my mind was being developed in a variety of ways.

I remember the smells, tastes, feelings, and sounds of those celebratory moments. Those memories bring me closer to that little boy I'm in a frantic search for as I now look for deliverance from a debilitating crack cocaine addiction I've fought off and on since I retired from the military in 1999.

Overall, I had a loving childhood with many different stories of experiences that could never be written, but in deliverance through the window of my mind, it was necessary for me to go back and recapture memories to identify the good and innocent times that helped in molding me with tenacity and a can-do spirit.

TWO

SPIRITUAL FATHER, A WATCHMAN ON THE WALL

I would be derelict in my duty to explain who, what, and how I am without mentioning a character who took center stage in my life. This spiritual personality was and still is undeniably a force that reckons within me mindfully as I search for who I was and who I truly am and as I examine today's recent dilemmas with the hope of who I'll be today and tomorrow. I now look back meditatively in desirous mindfulness to recapture the thoughts that gave a vision of who I'd like to be in matters of the heart where God resides.

God's work by his Spirit led this man. God's gift of grace provided the powered ability to disarm and transform the atmosphere from darkness into God's marvelous light. This man chose his plan for coverage from the one and only true God's Trinitarian essence. I know now who and what he was following that gave this appeared strength in my eyes and the gift to teach without pen and paper. The walk of this six-foot-six man taught and gave credence to the anointing impartation he possessed. This anointing was given by God, and I could see it as he went about living his life. This man was a friend of my father's. This man was a friend to my family. This man was just plain friendly. I remember his ability to be around the unsaved with the powered patience to intermittently bring about change without compromising his own beliefs. I saw this man create an atmosphere for the saved to freely show and deliberately project indiscretions by thought, word, and deed without fear of condemnation or judgment. I could see the understanding love in his eyes. I could feel his discernment of the sins of fathers long ago being perpetuated in the moments of encounter. He would make no mention of it at the time, but he would compartmentalize his approach as he was led by the Spirit of God.

The name of this man was Pastor John L. Shaw. He was, at the time of my awareness, the pastor of Saint John AME Church on the west side of Kansas City, Missouri. He would pull up in front of our house, and as he would open his door, his imposing figure would gradually ascend fully out of the car. I watched him as he walked up to the house with enormous strides. He quickly appeared in the doorway. My father or mother would let him in. He had a thunderous voice with distinction not to be compared, and he greeted the entire family with exceeding joy and love.

His vocabulary often left me in awe and sometimes without understanding the full conversations, which began with verbal banter and laughs and transitioned into a display of a higher mindset with sincerity coupled with commanding use of the English language. In the pulpit, as he preached, I was often puzzled by his large arsenal of meaningful words, which I coveted in my perception of my near and distant future. I began studying words, practicing speaking, and acting to be in school and church plays.

Reverend John L. Shaw put a lasting impression on most of my family and most of the people aforementioned in the cozy little house I described. John would, on occasion, come to my grandmother's house after Sunday service and eat with us, and I remember some of the false pretenses from a few as they attempted to project forms of righteousness without necessity because of John's nonjudgmental condition of acceptance for all he'd encountered. I would just laugh inside, as I could see the masks being removed after his departure from the cozy little house.

In the first seventeen years of my life, I had up-front, close, and personal encounters with this great man. He led me to Christ, he baptized me, and he encouraged me to take part in the youth ministries of not only the churches he pastored but the entire AME fifth district in Kansas City. He had me participating in vacation Bible school, and I was not the only youth he encouraged and influenced. He had my entire family participating, including my sister-cousin Sherita Williams.

My biggest memories of John L. Shaw were formed at a church called Gilbert Memorial AME in the Leeds area of Kansas City, where most of my meaningful experiences with Christianity transpired. Reverend Shaw was transferred from Saint John AME to pastor Gilbert Memorial AME, where I met families and friends I will hold dear for the rest of my life.

At that little old church, my knowledge of God increased. It was an old white wooden church with stairs that led up to the front entrance. There we would enter the sanctuary, and upon entry, we encountered squeaking wooden floors and wooden benches separated by an aisle between them. At the front of the church was the kneeling altar, where we received communion. The communion table that held the sacraments and spiritual artifacts was centered directly behind the altar. For years, we received these ceremonious sacraments at that altar, knelt and prayed, and were prayed for by elders and Reverend John L. Shaw.

The pulpit was a platform up from the altar, with two steps on each side to enter the pulpit. The pulpit held three chairs, with the pastor's chair directly centered behind the podium. To the left and right of the pulpit were the musical instruments played by Mrs. Mason.

There were two small rooms located in the instrumental areas. By the organ was the room that housed administrative material, with all the supplies for the sacraments. By the piano, the finance room did its supernatural acts for the church.

The choir stand was located directly behind the pulpit, with five wooden benches placed upon ascending platforms, which allowed all to see the choir members. The old church had a basement that I was afraid of, and I hoped no one would ever ask me to go there by myself.

Shortly after my family and I became established within the new church family, John showed me a new facet of himself that I was unfamiliar with. He got the church to agree to build a new church right next to the existing structure. I began to see him not just as a builder in the spiritual realm of God by his works displayed but also as a builder in the physical realm.

I didn't see the vision upon announcement of the new church, but in the gradual process, I began to see the vision coming to fruition.

It began with footers, the foundation, and exposed plumbing, followed by the slab. At that point, I still couldn't see the vision, but John could, because he was with the contractors every step of the way. He was in on the measurements, which he specified on the blueprints. Weeks passed before the framing for the concrete walls was built, after the slab dried and cured.

John was still up close and personal with the details as he stood and watched the contractors' progress. After the walls' frames laced with barbed wire were placed and the concrete was poured into the wall frames, a phase I had been unable to see appeared.

Now it was time for the headers and floor support for the first floor, and John L. Shaw was still involved every step of the way. I witnessed him verbally joust with the contractors for more expediency and with knowledgeable suggestions that would save time and costs on the building project.

After the floor and walls were built, we began adding cinder block. This stage required that the youth of Gilbert Memorial AME get involved by carrying cinder blocks and placing them in the hands of the older men of the church to erect. Some had skills already, and the teachings of John helped those who were in the learning stage.

That phase, with the supervision of John, cut the cost of the building of the church structure, as it allowed the contractors to skip that phase and return the next week with equipment to hoist the support beams and material for the roof.

At that point, I began to see a portion of the vision I was part of. I had no idea I was part of something that would outlast my time on earth and be impactful many years after my spiritual transition or ascension.

With the finished frame, completed roof, and electrical wiring in place, I really became impressed with the vision. John the builder was no longer in need of the construction company; he began subcontracting skilled carpenters and laborers under his supervision.

That phase lasted for quite some time as we still held Sunday service in the old church next to the new structure. John the builder micromanaged the delicate details that remained to complete the aesthetic beauty of the new and beautiful but small church. I look back now at what I didn't see then, and I find that John the builder had a high rating of efficacy in a myriad of categories, especially life.

As the building of the church came to its final phase, John became even more scrupulous as we began building the pulpit and choir stand. The youth of the church were intricately involved at that juncture of the tedious process. I worked closely with Reverend Shaw, and he taught me how to cut measurements while he nailed the cut pieces into place. I couldn't see the finished work of all the cuts, and no one to this day can see something I added to every cut I made: I used a marker to write my name on every two-by-four placed on the right side of the altar and pulpit. To this day, the marking cannot be seen by anyone. Only Terry and Floyd Randolph could possibly remember this, and one other person took it to his grave without mention: John Shaw himself.

Reverend asked me while I was writing on the boards, "Why are you writing on the boards?"

Thinking of the building possibly lasting past my time, I said, "I want to be remembered for being part of building this church."

I thought I was going to be chastised, as if I were practicing the art of graffiti on a sacred structure. However, that expected response was only a figment of my imagination, for John's response pertained only to time, in reference to my cutting and handing him pieces to put in place. I figured out a system due to his instruction of "I need twelve cuts at a particular measurement." I sped up the process of cutting and writing my name.

I waited with great anticipation for his next order of instruction, to continue placing my name on each cut. At the completion of the beautiful edifice, a huge portion transpired in a cycle or season of my life, without my foresight of the future events that would be integral in shaping my evolving identity. The experience of building that church, family and friends, and that man had a great impact on my life, and the spiritual residue persists today.

When John would show up at my grandmother's cozy house with my family, I could see his real humanity, despite his beliefs. In every encounter, whether in the neighborhood, the store, the gas station, the church, or that cozy little house, I could see the nonbeliever, the believer, the practicing believer, the self-righteous believer, and the never-practiced-and-not-intending-to-practice believer encounter saintly, sanctified John L. Shaw. I can now look back and see that in the Spirit, he had a gift to dismantle and decimate atmospheres of condemnation that existed.

The honorable John L. Shaw showed me how to take an idea, thought, hope, or dream out of my head and into manifestation. I've experienced this in the physical realm, and I now want to duplicate it in the spirit realm.

Through John L. Shaw and in my grandmother's house, in which I learned to rub love and affections in the tiny pathways of life, I learned how to be cool, gained the desire to do well in school, learned how to be respectful, learned how to be slick in the streets, and learned the essence of God. I learned many facets of my life from relationships, death, family, the effects of abusing drugs and alcohol, and other adversities. In those experiences in life, I learned forgiveness, patience, tolerance, religion, education, love, and spirituality. I attained my outlook and philosophies on life. Through these memories and experiences encountered in my genesis as a young man, I attempt to rebuild upon the solid foundation laid before me in the beginning. I will use them mindfully to be delivered through the window of my mind.

THREE

IN THE MIDST OF MY GENESIS

I can now tell you about experiences along the way that will give you deeper insight into the title of this book, *Deliverance through the Window of My Mind.*

Everyone gains a mental psyche created by what I consider the wheel of life. I call it a wheel because of its ability to roll as a wheel disguised by time, despite the seasonal terrains in life. When I found life to be easy or good, my wheel seemed to be rolling downhill without impediment or restriction as I kept my eyes on the prize, in which I could find some sense of certainty. When I found life to be difficult, the direction of my life seemed to change into a mirage of mountains camouflaged as hills, with various steep ascensions. I'd look to acquire a grip, thinking, *Why is life so hard? I can't make it; I can't do it mentality.* When I found life to be melancholy or bland, my wheel seemed to be on a flat surface yet with a gravitational pull of time that kept moving me forward toward the inevitable fate that lay in wait, whether it was good or bad.

I've faced times of fear, trauma, sadness, depression and grief, darkness, impending storms with clouds that appeared like difficulties, uncertainty, and glimpses of destruction, and I've survived. I now realize that these things too shall pass, and I hold close to the beliefs proven empirically by my perceived understanding of blue skies holding the sun as it radiates renewal in our existence in the physical as well as the spiritual realm. I also experienced times of happiness born of joy, times of gratitude measured by grace and mercy, times when love for me and the love I had for others were paramount in my thinking, and times when all that was good made the negative things in life meaningless. I was raised in the church, and I attributed the many blessings upon me and my family to God. I don't tell anyone which God or higher power to have faith in; however, whatever your belief, one thing that I know without doubt is constant for all existence is time. If you believe nothing else, know that time waits for nobody; it continues without interruption by any deity of choice.

As I look back over the portions of my life that stand out with distinction, I find them tied to the title of this book, *Deliverance through the Window of My Mind*, for it was God in my mind who held me together for many years. It was God who held me through all my trauma and pain. However, when I came into the grips of, or fell prey to, a debilitating drug addiction to crack cocaine, I found a season of night that blinded me and put muffs on my ears to impede my hearing from God.

Not only did I have to go back and find that little boy from my beginning, but I had to use my senses and memory of my senses of sound, taste, smell, sight, and touch to retrieve myself and redirect myself.

By writing therapeutics, I have hoped to fix my future and find the strength to heal my past. In writing therapeutics, I'm thankful for the numbing effect of those bad memories, which I also write about but never will forget.

I'll go back to a time in my life when I remember living without a care in the world because I knew, or was aware of, only the beauty of the sunshine in blue skies and the fullness of the bright moon in dark skies, surrounded by sparkling lights that I know now to be stars. I remember the changing formations of white smoke that drifted through the air effortlessly, which I know now to be clouds. I found beauty in the colors of the trees, flowers, and grass in my nonintentional, iniquitous state of being.

I heard the sounds of birds chirping, the wings of the bees as they traveled to and from the many arrays of flowers that caught my eye, and the flies as they pestered without prejudice. Squirrels scampered up and down and through the trees as their claws gave an expected visual through the leaves that camouflaged their silhouettes. In the summer, armies of ants would cross the sidewalk on the walkway leading out of our yard, and being a kid, I would stomp on as many as I could, trying to kill them all, with little to no success, in my nonintentional, iniquitous state of being. I would watch and wait in the summer for the magical light show displayed by the lightning bugs. It would sometimes be gradual, and at times, they'd be like the army of ants but in the air. Being a kid, I would try to catch or kill every one of them, to no avail. I'd soon be content and tired of the futile efforts, and we'd gather to compare the amount and sizes as the light show continued all around us in my nonintentional, iniquitous state of being.

The four seasons brought distinguishable memories stored by smell, feel, sight, and activity. The summer held most of the memories, which included, along with the aforementioned, racing bicycles, playing all forms of sports, going on adventures in the woods, having adventures along the streams, building tents, and making go-karts. We'd progressively create unimaginable fun in my nonintentional, iniquitous state of being.

The fall season began with the change of colors and temperature and the smell of green death, which brought about a different form of activity in fun and work with the falling of the leaves.

I ask you to utilize your mind to picture memorized senses by feel, sight, and smell of past seasons in the window of your mind.

In winter, snow changed the environment of play, sound, smell, and feel, bringing snowball fights, the creation of snow angels and snowmen, and the duration to endure cold temperatures until they became unbearable. At that breaking point, individual tolerance led me to go inside, seeking the solace of heat. I remember the smell of shoveling snow with dry, frozen leaves underneath, and the wet leaves also gave a noticeable smell, depending on the temperature of the sun.

Spring had a profound and culminating effect on the outlook of life, as it repeatedly gave indication of a myriad of things coming back to life or new forms that could be seen, heard, and smelled.

Now I use these memories metaphorically to aid in the newly perceived vision of deliverance through the window of my mind. I sit and wonder if these seasons can bring bridges for crossings for all of us to go back and find mental strength. I tied my fluctuating seasons of life to negative or positive decisions and the natural repercussion of life in general. The only constant was change, for better or worse.

Many view cloudy days as dreary and seemingly uncomfortable because of the absence of the sun and variations of rainfall. I now go to deliverance through the window of my mind with a visual of my first plane flight on a dreary, cloudy day. With the ascending of the plane in the dark, cloudy sky, a new visual appeared that changed my perspective of the cloudy-day syndrome. I could feel the power of the sun. I could also see the power of the sun in a perfect blue sky that stretched unendingly. In this moment in time, I now attribute the many experiences of life, whether good or bad, to the power of God above the cloudy days.

I now go back in my mind to recapture that little boy. I need desperately to regain that nonintentional state of being, when I didn't intend on sinning but sinned. I now know that sinful strongholds with intent of gratifying fleshly desires are intentional states of being with consequences, repercussions, and imminent destructions of our bodies and our souls in the spiritual realm and the physical realm. Now my addiction recovery gives me a comparison or a measurement, like the weighing of a scale, for the mustering of strength or power to surmount and overcome this drug spirit. This spirit is my giant, my kryptonite, and is leading me into my own exodus through the window of my mind.

FOUR

IN THE MIDST OF TRAUMA AND TRIUMPHS OR GOOD AND BAD

D istinctly, I remember painful moments of the past that hurt and left mental scars lingering like permanent fixtures hung from the centers of my mind. Emphatically, at the same time, I remember and hold on to exhilarating experiences and moments that gave unspeakable joy with a vision filled with hope and certainty of better days to come. Those experiences created who I am today. I attribute my unique personality to those traumas and triumphs. We all have uniqueness in our personalities, according to or dependent on the environments that fostered our experiences in life. With the traumas and triumphs, our personalities become like fingerprints that can only be extracted by the supernatural Creator, who knew us before this consciousness of ourselves and before we had any resemblance to who we are today. In this book, I'm trying to manifest who I'd like to be in my tomorrows.

Most of us describe this supernatural entity as God, despite our beliefs and inability to describe the entity with words. This supernatural entity, with powers unbeknownst to me, possesses knowledge down to the smallest details, such as knowing the number of hairs on my head and knowing the thoughts I think before I myself know the origination for a conceived thought. This is the description attributed by mankind to the all-knowing, all-powerful, omnipresent, supernatural entity. I'm extremely eager to aggrandize gratefully this supernatural entity in my belief system that I identify with and claim as light onto my soul.

In this book, you will draw no criticism from me, nor will you have judgment from me, due to my faith and understanding of the supernatural entity who still covers me in my iniquitous state of being. My choice is God and his Spirit of truth. It is God to me, this supernatural presence only recognizable in my heart. While applying these principles of Spirit and truths in myself mindfully and in human atmospheres, I appear deliberately and unintentionally wherever I may be. I give complete credence to God for perfecting that great work in me, which he began in me a long time ago.

In my beginning state, my unintentional-iniquities state of being, I now compare my spiritual and physical existence in this time in my life as God continues to nurture my spirit in his wombed creation of time.

In the trauma and the devastating memories of such traumas, I become entrenched in a vicious cycle of rehashing pain. I use small hurts to feel a form of pain less offensive than the original sensations encountered. I write with the expectation of being recovered and in deliverance through the window of my mind. I now rely upon my writing to soothe those moments affected by such trauma in my existence.

It is in the triumphs in my life that gave me a true sense of victory, with a blueprint or road map to duplicate this power of grace I define as supernatural power. I find that this supernatural power works best in my weakest state of being, helping me to do what I believed and felt was insurmountable. There have been times in my life when situations looked impossible, yet I found myself overcoming them.

I now look back through the window of my mind to solidify pictorial memories, good or bad, into the stone tablets of my heart and on the frontlets of my spiritual eye. I now use Brian Edward Dixon's self-proclaimed philosophy of using my mind as a window to create an atmosphere indicative of a fruit haven consisting of love, joy, grace, and mercy. I've familiarized my subconscious with that which is good to assist my conscious state of being in setting the boundaries to make sound choices. I do this to avoid suffering due to the possible acceptance of my sentient consciousness's dabbling in any intentional iniquitous states of being that can lead me to a destination under hell and result in misfortunes or curses visited upon generations of my offspring.

I now look back on a few things I'll share regarding trauma and triumph. My first remembered trauma was at about four years old. I was running from something and ran right into the edge of a door. It may have been hours later when I woke up and found myself under an obscure netting inside a small playpen-like bed. I could hear the voices of my mother and auntie discussing my condition, and for the first time in my life, I pondered my physical condition of tomorrow with uncertainty.

Another trauma occurred about five years later, when the children of Saint John AME were in a schoolyard across from the church, playing on the playground. I was on the monkey bars with my sister Kim, and Kim and I noticed a man slowly edge his way toward us. I began to discern his intent as he walked under the monkey bars, gazing upward intently at the girls as they played on the monkey bars. He then suddenly made his move, and upon recognition of what was happening and the screaming of my sister, everyone ran toward the church, screaming, as I witnessed the man carry my sister to the side of the building to evade being seen. I followed him and began to posture as if to intimidate him into stopping his intended assault. He just looked at me and said, "Little boy, go away before you get hurt."

As he laid my sister on the ground, I could still hear the commotion of the others trying to tell an adult at the church what was going on. I saw him go under my sister's clothing. I immediately got close and out of his peripheral vision to inflict pain on his back. He winced and began swinging backward at me as he continued to assault my sister. I continued hitting him with everything I could conjure at that moment in my adrenaline-fueled state. I may have deterred his complete desire of satisfaction, but he still inflicted a lifelong affliction of trauma upon my sister. His plans were foiled, and he got up and ran, narrowly escaping the men of the church. My trauma was in not saving my sister from that experience, and it still haunts me till this day.

Another experience I consider triumph through trauma occurred when a young man by the nickname of Doc Savage, who was feared by many, appeared at Mary Harmon Weeks Grade School to inflict pain on some of my friends. I remember the sound of his clothing as he scaled the fence, dressed in a karate suit and carrying nunchucks. The sound was memorable due to all the karate movies I watched with my big brother Darren. That sound was like that of sheets hanging on a clothesline on a windy day. Upon landing from the top of the fence, Doc Savage walked slowly toward my friends as he spewed threats that scared the entire crowd. I, not liking bullies, interjected by asking Doc Savage to leave the guys alone. I figured that because Doc Savage was my neighbor who lived across the street from me, he would listen to my plea for peace. However, it made matters worse.

He turned his attention toward me as he got closer to me. I was shaking in my shoes with fear while holding a lamppost that had been made in the industrial arts class at Martin Luther King Junior High School. Doc Savage continued to get closer until I could smell his foul breath as I was backed into the same fence he'd jumped. I asked him to back away from me, but he persisted, and the crowd noise rose. I went into automatic mode and swung as hard as I could, striking him on the right side of his head. Instantaneously, blood began to ooze from his head.

Doc Savage collapsed as the crowd conveyed astonishment while scattering from the scene. I too ran with fear, thinking that this was not the end of old Doc Savage. A few minutes and a few blocks away, the sound of alert was again lifted by many, as Doc Savage, now holding a gigantic boulder over his head, called my name. I glanced and saw his bloodstained karate suit and gauged his pursuit pace quickly.

Inundated with fear, I ran but not in the most direct route. I deviated due to Doc Savage's known ability to run fast, and I disbelieved I could make it home via a direct route. I made a hard left and ran until known paths of the past presented themselves. I ran through backyards and jumped fences, getting to different blocks, trying to get closer to home. The crowd noise dissipated, and silence gave me a since of security, yet fear persisted. That led me into another fear I found acceptable: I have a strong aversion to dogs, caused by previous attacks. It didn't matter at that point, due to the greater fear of Doc Savage. I saw a doghouse and intended to enter it, only to find a dog inside. It immediately began to sniff and lick me. I didn't know the dog's intentions and didn't care as long as he refrained from barking, as I thought it would give away my position. I stayed there until I thought it was safe enough to wind my way home to safety.

It was about an hour before I came out to now take the most deliberate way to my house. I came to the house directly behind mine, went through their backyard, and jumped my final fence to my backyard. I saw people in front of my house from the driveway eaves of my house, so I chose the opposite side of my house to jump onto the porch. I now had a full visual of the spectators, and at the bottom of the steps leading up to my house sat Doc Savage with a bandage wrapped around his head, now dressed in a black trench coat, as he waited for my return to my house. Gasps from people gathered alerted Doc Savage, and he spotted me as I was putting my hands on the handle of the screen door.

Narrowly, I escaped as I entered my house and shut the door. I viewed Doc Savage walk up to the front door. I was relieved momentarily when my brother Darren, the karate master who just wanted to kick somebody's ass, greeted me as I turned to go up the stairs to my room. Darren blocked my way and gave me two choices: go out there to face Doc Savage or take a beatdown from him. I reluctantly chose to face Doc, for my chance with Darren was apparent.

I began to shake in my shoes. I looked out the window at the people gathered and opened the door as Doc moved to the house next door, which had an open yard. Everyone circled to spectate.

I asked my brother to manage the rules of the impending fight by telling Doc he couldn't use karate. Darren told me to just go fight.

I walked into the midst of the circle, where Doc took off his trench coat. Underneath was a new karate suit with shoes to match. I looked at Darren and implored him to instruct Doc not to use karate in the fight, but to no avail. I turned and faced my opponent, and he went into a karate stance with a noise to accompany his posture. I put my hands up as he came toward me. I wanted to run, but the thickness of the moment didn't allow any thinking about escape. Doc grabbed me and flipped me as he gave a thunderous blow to my back that sounded like the crash of a diver jumping from a one-hundred-foot diving board and accidentally committing a belly buster, giving the impression of imminent death. The crowd again lifted a sound of astonishment with a hint of doom.

I could feel the damage to my ego persisting until the end of time and found a quiet place in my mind that had no fear of any kind. I got up and began jabbing Doc one punch at a time as he made dramatic moves and sounds that had intimidated me just moments before. I then slowed my mind down some more and began two-punch and three-punch combinations until Doc's look of confidence disappeared as if from a magician's sleight-of-hand routine.

I was still feeling a sense of vindication denied from running with fear, hiding in a doghouse with fear, and having my brother make me face my fear while basically saying, "Don't be a punk." I found the culmination of those events to be unacceptable. I now look back at this experience and attribute it to the title of this book, *Deliverance through the Window of My Mind.*

I could see, at that moment in life, the damage to my persona by the notorious Doc Savage. I felt that even if I won the battle, my reputation was unrepairable. Then I entered an out-of-body experience that showed me how to get back all that had been taken from me. I saw the thoughts of me I wanted to be projected being renewed to others but especially Doc. I saw a peace within me that could be measured by courage despite the outcome of the experience. I saw a different level of desperation taking me into a realm to rewrite the narrative of my could've-been past into my will-be future.

Doc, with shock, turned and ran toward his house across the street as I pursued him, hitting him in the back of his head. I sensed a need to solidify a message that needed no questions from the people who went away with a story that could last through the annals of time. I sought to take that which could've been taken from me in the respect of my manhood, which I would desperately need to maneuver in the neighborhood I lived in. People's perception of me is and will always be important to me. I beat Doc all the way into his house, where he lay face down while I continued to beat him in the back as I talked to him, giving warning about the next time of confrontation.

I've carried this event and others as visual reminders in life, hoping to recognize that in this physical realm or in the spiritual realm, things may be seemingly insurmountable, causing you to doubt the possibility of overcoming the tribulations sure to come and to put your hands up in the air as if waving a white flag of surrender for all to see. I didn't know at the time that this trauma experience could be used in titling this book *Deliverance through the Window of My Mind*.

I consider experiences of trauma and triumph to be lessons to learn from. In the remembrance of joy in our lives, successes in our lives, and pain in times past, we can re-create the moments by familiarity with expectations of a desired outcome.

In experiences of trauma, pain, and grief of tragedies, I've learned to remember "This too shall pass, and I will breathe again." It is not for me to wonder why, find answers to questions that are unanswerable, or fix the pains of yesterday, but it is up to me to face the realities of life, moving on by not being stuck in pains of the past. This is what I call being delivered through the window of the mind.

When I got to Hope by the Sea for my debilitating drug addiction to crack cocaine, I met a man named Frank Buffa, who helped me to get past a horrific trauma of my past. The complexity of this trauma wasn't in facing fear or triumph through success; it was in the acceptance of things I could never change.

Distant but not faint was the murder of my little brother Brent Joseph Dixon. It threw my entire family into disbelief in individualistic manners that cannot be explained. In times before, a repetitive cycle of creating a visual of Brent's last moments was uppermost in my mind. Was he cold? To what extent was his fear? Did he wish I were there to protect him? Did he know he was going to die? In repetitive cycles, I'd create different outcomes to save him by being there, while punishing myself for not being there. In times before, my inquisitiveness about who would do such a thing, why they would do it, and why the police couldn't solve the murder of my brother drove me into a paranoia that existed for years. This paranoia was compartmentalized by my thinking that one day, the person or persons responsible would be right in my face, talking with me, and I wouldn't have a clue.

At Hope by the Sea, in Frank Buffa's class, through written assignments about this experience and many more, I finally came to peace through acceptance. I used Frank's methods with a variety of memories of traumas and successes of my past, and now I write about my expected future to find deliverance through the window of my mind. I can now be delivered from my past hurts, pains, and disappointments by facing them and transferring them from my mind onto a piece of paper with a mental dialogue with an expected end. I can now also create a future through my mind by a vision of hope and desire acceptable to God. It is not about our material substance; it is about prioritizing spiritual substance and allowing the God of provision to add materials that we can't explain or contain.

FIVE

MOVING TOWARD DARKNESS

n September 1999, I retired from the military at the age of thirty-nine without a clue of what lay ahead for me. Less than thirty days after taking off my uniform, I began the opening of Pandora's box. I felt unfulfilled after a purposeful past and the unexpected success of retirement at a young age. Once the box was halfway open, I found myself addicted to crack cocaine. I began to squirm for help and relief, but to no avail. I began to think I could tame the tiger of addiction, but it kept eating my lunch. It kept taking my hope; it took my morals and integrity. I couldn't keep a job, I began a season of isolation, and I started to see my relationships with the ones I loved deteriorate like a corpse sure to come. I tried everything within my power at the time to break free from my addiction. I developed a love-hate relationship, which gave me the power of pause, with a pumping-of-the-brakes effect. The power of pause was useful at times but ineffective. It is only a moment in time of abstaining from the murdering spirit of addiction, which casts a shadow that can't be seen but is sure to follow. The shadow of my addiction was on me like a blanket on a cold winter night. I found myself outside my house, dressed in a three-piece suit of shame, guilt, and embarrassment. I would ride past my house several times without the intestinal fortitude to use my key to open the door.

There was a time when this Pandora's box seemed locked open on metal hinges rained on and rusted through the annals of time. I was changing the boundaries I once had set for myself in the past amid my successes. That which had been unimagined and unacceptable became part of my realized reality.

I now visualized my addiction as a woman. I remembered men in the past who would cheat on their wives and had another family or girlfriend across town. I felt I was married to two women, and the unneeded wife of addiction was living right next door. I could hear the voice of this addiction calling as I lay next to my real wife. I could see the addiction wife next door in her conditioned patience, always waiting for me to appear outside my house. I often heard her call my name, as if I didn't remember I had a relationship with her too. I'd wonder sometimes if my real wife could hear the voice of my addiction wife next door insisting I come out to play.

I now visualize my addiction wife as the prettiest woman in the world, and I, being starved of physical attention, waited and watched her as she appeared. I thought we had an exclusive relationship, but as I looked around, I could see her being intimate with many people around me. I'd wait and watch her appear without any mental combativeness or reservation of her infidelity, and as she lay in pose, I could feel a physical gulp in my throat that I made plans to resist or avoid to lessen the anticipation of the first hit, in order not to lose control.

In preparing myself to approach, I could see smoke coming from between her legs. That gave me cause to pause, but my mental dependency and physical desire couldn't accept the evidence, so

I'd step closer. Upon further examination, I could see green stuff oozing from between her legs, but in my iniquitous state of being, with my mental prowess still getting the best of me, I'd step closer, now visualizing maggot-like bugs, seemingly on steroids, circling the dark hole, emitting a sound like a three-day-old corpse without a casket, buried above ground. I now visualized the self-gratifying pipe to be the representative escort assigned to deliver me into the kingdom of darkness with the intent to collect a handsome bounty. I, without pondering the devastating repercussions being imposed on my existence in spiritual and physical realities, began to fight for and by familiarities of my past perceived sentient being.

In my incredulous naivete, I positioned myself in a pandemic mode like in COVID. It reminded me of spreading an STD, but because it was drug addiction for me, I call it ATD: addictively transmitted disease. In active form, it affects the host and all who love and care about him or her while rendering his or her entire life useless even to him- or herself.

The constant love-hate relationship with both wives was taking a toll on me. My journey into the abyss of darkness had no resemblance to a planned round-way ticket. It was becoming apparent that this trip was a one-way ticket straight to hell. It was like going into a descending cave of caverns without leaving markers for a path I could return by.

The dark moments escalated. It would not be constructive in writing to inform you of the myriad negative experiences, but I find it necessary to point out the more memorable and impressionable moments of my captivity by addiction.

I found myself outside my house again during a long, cold winter, in another house that was even colder. This house had no running water and no legal electricity; it was powered by a gas generator. It had four cats without a litter box, and I could smell cat defecation before I came into the house. The house had a giant hole in the floor of the kitchen, which gave me the ability to investigate the basement, which was in desperate need of cleaning. I could see and feel bad spirits dwelling as they waited for instruction from Satan himself.

The moving of boundaries gave me a form of contentment to accept the physical, spiritual, and mental state of my existence as I cried deep inside for help. My addiction became ubiquitous, touching every important part of my life that I held sacredly within the boundaries of the past.

I once beheld the pain in my eldest son's eyes when he found me in that house. I had asked him to cut my hair and take me over to my grandfather's house to take a shower. It was the cozy little house of the past, but my grandmother was no longer physically there. My son then took me back to the homeless house and dropped me off. I could feel his pain the entire time he was in my presence, but I held the pain in his eyes as he pulled off. I saw the pain as I shut the car door. I saw the pain as he started the car. I saw the pain as he placed the car in gear. I held the full weight of his pain as I saw the look on his face in the rearview mirror, knowing he did not want to leave his daddy in that godforsaken condition.

I stayed in that house with two others until we were notified that the house was scheduled for demolition. We then moved directly across the street to a house the other two owned, which had been damaged by a fire set by someone months before I met them and moved into the house that was to be demolished. Their house had holes burned into the roof by the previous fire, no running water, no electricity, and no doors. Their house was in worse condition than the one we'd just left. I stayed there for about a week as my outlook on life continued to diminish into a deeper darkness. I could now locate the pain I was feeling, seated in the lowest region of my stomach. I could now feel the war that transpired between my flesh and my spirit. The pain was in my soul's being exposed to both heaven and hell at the same time.

I, not being of sound mind, decided to ask a drug dealer who had a form of respect for me if I could stay at one of his houses that he was preparing to sell the poison that had me bound. He agreed with stipulations hinging on my ability to help with reconstructing his home. I remembered some of the skills taught by John L. Shaw in the building of the church long ago, so I agreed.

We eventually got down to the security system and added metal screen doors, bars on all windows, and a camera and alarm system. Meanwhile, I was working on Sheetrocking and making a slot for transactions in the back of the house. We were trying to keep the house clean and placed sheets between the rooms to cut the Sheetrock dust produced by my work. I completed the slot in the back for a transaction that day, and we agreed to use it and stop letting people in.

I was in the bathroom, when I heard the doorbell. I heard a pleasant conversation when the door was opened, but suddenly, things turned bad. I heard a scuffle of violence with raised voices of demands. I heard the drug dealer insisting he had nothing as I felt the vibration and sound of the beating that was taking place.

I heard the robber say, "You know what this is. Where's it at?"

The drug dealer still insisted through his cries of pain that he had nothing. The robber then instructed his co-robber to go to the front of the house and check those rooms. The co-robber appeared past the first sheet hung to reduce dust, and I peered at him from the bathroom across the hall. I stood quietly and still with a pipe in one hand and a lighter in the other. I could hear his frantic search as he tossed the first bedroom's belongings to the drug dealer. He came out of that bedroom into the front room, which was located directly in front of the room just searched. I moved at an angle to prevent him from catching me peripherally, and I shadowed him from that angle, watching his searching method. I was still listening to the lead robber question the drug dealer while pistol-whipping him at the same time.

The search in the front of the house was seemingly complete, as I watched the intruder, with a pistol in hand, pull the sheet back and disappear from my sight. Seeing that moment in the blink of an eye with a variety of possible outcomes and scenarios, my mind expected and accepted death, and I decided to take my last hit on the pipe, filled with the spirit of death.

Meanwhile, the brutal assault continued for the drug dealer and on my mind at the same time. I'd previously, in moments of despair, thought it better to just die to get away from my undetachable addiction, but I had no courage to hurt myself, despite accepting my end by a truck running over my car to end the misery of my addiction. I didn't want to die a violent death, as my little brother Brent had, so my mind went into survival mode. I figured that moving to the bedroom that already had been searched was my best option at the time. I put my lighter and pipe on the sink with no expectation of ever hitting it again and quietly moved to the other room, under the cover of the sheets hung to reduce the spread of dust caused by my work.

I immediately went into the closet but still felt insecure, so I began to use tactics of camouflage to break the outline of my body as I sat at the bottom of the closet, underneath hanging clothes. I used dirty socks, underwear, and clothing to appear invisible as I sat quietly, barely breathing.

The lead robber continued to question the drug dealer as he beat him harder, but the words of the drug dealer were becoming muttered. The lead robber instructed his assistant to go check his room again. I could have died in fear of his coming presence. I saw him at the entrance of the closet with his left leg in the entryway and a gun in his left hand, about twelve inches from my face. He began using his right hand to go through the pockets of the clothing hanging directly above my head.

I saw the darkness of my addiction in a new light as my soul hovered in an out-of-body experience. I could see the ghost of the future—not speaking but pointing to what was to come. I pondered, in the moment, taking the gun; twisting it out of his hand; and turning it on him, but with hesitancy through quick visualizations of my death, I remained statue-like.

When his search was complete, his menacing figure disappeared from the entryway of the closet I continued to sit in. I then heard the voice of the drug dealer faintly say, "It's in the basement."

I heard a door open and felt the weight and vibrations as the robber hit every step on his way down. I could hear the quick tossing of the basement, until I heard him say with excitement, "I found it!"

The beating momentarily came to a halt as they examined their find. They finally left but not without delivering their last words accompanied by the last blow of a shot that still rings within my memory till this day.

The increasing darkness came a few days later as the brothers of the drug dealer came over, and we discussed retaliation. I agreed to take part; I felt my participation was necessary due to the way I'd felt while hiding in the closet. I was now entering a reprobate state of mind, because God was no longer in my thoughts. I found it acceptable to shoot and possibly kill another human being just to feel vindicated. I now visualize in hindsight the devil dispatching numerous small imps to accost me while putting me on my knees with my butt in air. The devil himself appeared, descending slowly and then approaching directly behind me. With a surprise of inward thrusts and with intent of no recovery from the damage inflicted physically, he sought to capture my soul. He didn't have the decency to apply lubricant to ease the excruciating pain that persisted in my rehashed memories of disappointment and fears of losing myself. He didn't even have the civility to offer a forewarned opportunity to use a reach-around for possible relief to minimize the vision of my spirit man dying. I was unable to further protect my soul, which was being exposed to heaven and hell simultaneously.

Three days later, my second-eldest son called me to express his concerns about me. He didn't know the details of my addiction, but what he was feeling led him to call me. I'm thankful for that call because it forced me into another direction. I began to see that all my children had invested interest in my well-being. I began to see the importance of my presence and no longer wanted to be rendered useless by a substance I was addicted to and held captive by.

I gathered myself and most of my belongings and managed to get a bus ticket from Kansas City to Atlanta, Georgia, where I had four years of abstaining from my addiction. I had another bout, but in 2019, the darkness of my addiction appeared like a shadow, looking for a host. The demons were multiplied by seven, and I could feel the reprobation returning. I visualized being on an elevator and pushing the up button to get above captivity, but the floor changes on the display moved in a downward motion. The speed of the downward motion accelerated, as if the cable of my life were broken. I frantically tried repetitive jumping motions, anticipating contact with the bottom, to avoid what seemed like imminent death. Time was of the essence, and what I was trying to do was not working, so I came up with an alternative plan to exit the downward elevator of my addiction by busting out straight ahead, no matter the possible position of the in-between floors of demise. I had to take a chance on catching a ledge straight ahead or below and holding on. The visualization of holding on was the representation of getting back on the throne provisioned by God for my rightful standing as the king and high priest of my family.

There were two dreams. From these visual dreams, I would wake up in a confused state, feeling that I hadn't finished or accomplished the most important feats of the past. I dreamed that I was missing credits to graduate from high school and that I never walked across the stage to receive my diploma. In the other dream, I didn't finish my time in the military to retire with a pension at the age of thirty-nine. I felt as if I were in the twilight zone. If this were real or true, my fight to regain hope from my debilitating addiction seemed insurmountable. I'd rehash the memories of time and effort put forth to secure those two levels of success in my life. I was deliberate and intentional, and I expected to have a positive outcome. That passion for better days to come was in the good portions of my upbringing, and a hunger to escape the misfortunes of a dysfunctional community heavily weighed on my mind. Staying home would have turned out to be planned obsolescence in commerce, and that drove my desperation not to become a statistic.

If this were real or true, then what about the deliberate and intentional efforts put forth to raise my children to be kind, loving, spiritual beings and to perpetuate this cycle in their offspring from experience? If this were true, I would be even more devastated.

I felt as if I were practicing self-mutilation and dying of a thousand cuts from the hits from the pipe. I felt as if a school of sharks in the ocean smelled blood and were waiting patiently for me to enter the water to get to the other side of my addiction, only to devour me as I attempted to navigate the gulf to recovery. The same visualization that led me to depart the descending elevator between floors pushed me into a desperation that led to a new and effective visualization of a deer panting for water after a near-miss shot from a hunter created a flight-or-fight mode into the abyss of nothingness. That nothingness direction was futile because its life was going to end by the hunter or lack of water.

What's real about escaping or being delivered from any addiction of any kind is the starting position. I see two islands separated by a tempestuous and tumultuous sea, with swirling winds producing violent waves. I inhabit the island of addiction, where the sun refuses to shine, hope refuses to exist, and low dark clouds persist. Yes, I, through my addiction, inhabit this island, where the shackles of my decisions have me bound. I long to be free, but I can't see how I'm going to get across the sea. I know this much: the storms of my addiction will keep raging, and I'll keep longing to get to the other shore, where I can see the light. There is no boat coming; there is no search party in the air. I must go into the mind, jump into the water of recovery, and take one stroke at a time, until I find myself on the other shore filled with the light of the world. I'm afraid of the repercussions of my addiction, which caused the self-mutilation that now oozes the blood needed for this journey across the sea of recovery. I know the sharks smell the opportunity of a feast, but I'm desperate in my leap into this journey of recovering my life. I will practice medicine without a license, for I've diagnosed the darkness of my addiction, and now I must have a prognosis for my addiction with light. I must put it to bed and say night-night!

SIX

MOVING TOWARD
THE LIGHT

n the previous chapter, I gave a proportioned and compartmentalized description of my pandemic-like addiction, confirmed by the diagnosed darkness, that resulted from my choice to self-gratify by adding to my plate a substance that led me into a comprehensive addiction. In moving toward the light, I can surely say I'm reminded daily of these repercussions. Like the sun's and moon's sameness in giving light and darkness, so was my dilemma up and down. I receptively stay mindful of the provisions of grace and mercy that kept me in my weakened state of addiction, while continuously remembering the pain. I cautiously examine my thoughts to realize my thinking. I tediously examine my shortcomings to realize my other flaws and iniquities that give credence to physical and spiritual strongholds that captivate us, take us to places we never intended to go to, and confine and keep us longer than we would ever agree to stay. In my self-conviction, I can honestly say this destination was never desired as a place to appear, and upon arrival, I can say from the bottom of my heart with contrition that I sincerely apologize to God and all those I hurt, even myself. I regretfully remember that season when considering the possibility of that being my life's outcome, with natural catastrophes in life lying gently ahead, bringing more than enough pain and traumatic experiences. This has become the thorn in my side that I ask to have taken from me in this physical realm, as I'm reminded of the pain and uncertainty of this self-imprisonment with bars that never lock.

I now place upon the frontlets of my eyes scriptures of light mixed with new forms of meditation proven effective. I use writing as a therapy. I've developed visualization techniques through apperception to increase my strength mentally and spiritually. I display stick-to-itiveness one day at a time and resolve to be able to see the light when it appears in the context of deliverance through the window of my mind. It is the only thing I can control. God has done all he needs to do to prove me, so I now look to grasp the power of this light. For me, this light requires a new template closing pathways to dark destinations awaiting my demise, depending on decisions made in my future.

In the previous chapter, I also gave a small prognosis of a needed comprehensive light to cure this debilitating disease that I and others tread upon: the high tightrope of addiction. As we teeter with the hope of a safety net proven nonexistent, we see many fall before our eyes, never to arise again. In my spirit man, I must now redefine the light I'm searching for, because it's become apparent that my perception of illumination has become distorted due to my subconscious contentment becoming evident as a result of addiction. This contentment spilled over into my conscious state of being, causing the manifestation of darkness, with reckless disarray, to appear while rendering uselessness as the destination and fate of my future. It's now evident that in my season of darkness, in my addiction, a fleshly, sophisticated dimmer switch was added to give me imitative lights. I confess and admit through contrition to those moments of imagined joy upon the high tightrope of my addiction in the presence of other good people teetering on high wires of darkness in altered states of mind—good people who helped to make some moments in that darkness appear brighter. In the moments of darkness, by this added dimmer switch, I ignored, without contrasting the variants of, this dark matter of light. This dimmer led me into a deeper, darker state of being with isolating doors that now swung two ways: I didn't want to be seen in the four walls of my darkness, and people didn't want to see me in my outward embracement of such darkness. I now feel that same added dimmer switch can be used for my good in turning up the light instead of turning it down.

I do know something about myself: I have the desire to be in the arena of joy, embracing people and things resembling forms of joy. I now notice the smiles of loving, kind people from then and now, and in the Spirit, I recognize inextinguishable sparkles of love in people's eyes. I recognize postures suggesting no need to fear. I recognize welcoming, luminous smiles of joys from the past and presently at Hope by the Sea. I again know something about myself in this process of deliverance through the window of my mind. I know about an out-of-body experience that allowed me to finally see myself through the eyes and minds of others and be comfortable with the description at a place called Hope by the Sea. Now, in an awakened state, I finally accept and receive the words spoken of me from the times of old. If the words spoken of me were a painting or a picture, it would show me as a blessed carrier of light, a good person with gifts and abilities to exhort others, an atmosphere changer with the willingness to place logs upon bonfires of love, joy, forgiveness, and prayer for deliverance and healing. I believe I can now receive and take hold of this compliment without fear of needed perfection, as in times past.

Through the window of my mind and moving toward the light, I add to myself the fire of reparative, sincere contrition because I find it imperative for my restoration. I now hear this sentiment about my goodness resurfaced in my weakened state as I continue projecting light into my existence till this day. In my awakened state, I also realize that at one time, as a little boy, I held a version of light once remembered in my unintentional state of sin. Considering the repercussions imposed as a result of my intentional sin, I'm encouraged by the ability to possess a light of hope to interject into the atmosphere of the hopeless, bringing forms of light consisting of joys. This newly imposed fire motivates me to look at myself impartially to expose to that self I often speak of and to others a form of transparency that gives away my power to define or control the narrative of myself to prevent exposure of that other self we all have a tendency to hide rather than truly expose, even to ourselves.

I now look for this light that illuminates all these bonfires, as I recognize the light bestowed upon me from the beginning of time. I look for the light in my successes in my past. I look for the Light who stood with me while I faced the many giants in the narrow pathways of my lifetime. I look for the Light who held me in the mist of trauma and sorrows in my lifetime. I look for the light I'm presently found in, held by immense gratitude's confining parameters of true light allowing me, at the moment, the sight of hope. I look for the Light who carried me through dangers seen and unseen. I look for the fire of light that continuously burns down deep in the pit of my soul, depicting the light of truth from the God I believe in. I now pant and thirst like a deer for water for the throne provisioned to me by God, for I, in his image, esteem myself to be a king and the high priest of my family, seeking to be rethroned.

I've listened to and observed the religious of many faiths. I've observed the practices of most, and they contain the same sorts of followers within their bodies of faith. I've heard from naysayers, nonbelievers, the misinformed, those who misinterpret scripture, those who manufacture ill-conceived spiritual intent, and those who become metamorphically cloaked in the entanglement of proselytism, with practices that include conversion by any means necessary, with death being acceptable. If not careful, we could subconsciously usurp the authority of God or any higher power we profess allegiance to. I'm starting to feel a bending of reality in our present moment in this time continuum. It appears illusion and delusion now sit at the table of our existence, and this disruption or unwanted guest has placed at our table uncertainty, with an aesthetic menu to lure the uninformed into this atmosphere of uncertainty we find ourselves in. I now stand on opposite sides of myself, cognizant of the projected images of my self's manifested beliefs gone wrong in times past. Tired and overburdened, I become desperate in my covetous heart's desire to remember the light of yesterday while in search of a much-needed new light for myself in the things concerning the flesh. Today I stand consuming the fallout of guiltiness that silenced the truth long ago. I now move toward this new light, and the closer I get, the more I feel my hands and feet being cleansed. As I approach this envisioned island of light, I can feel myself on the precipice of contact. I can feel the regeneration of true light illuminating again the pathways of transcendence awaiting each of us. It is important for us, as sentient beings, to inspect the items placed upon the tables of our lives, to avoid consuming servings of self-righteous piety characteristic of the Sadducees and the Pharisees of old, who were dripping with greed for power, jealous, and fearful of losing the minds of the followers while active in a distortion campaign to perpetuate an atmosphere of created delusions administered by illusionists providing a visual of sitting on the throne of judgment. They were intent on exacting control and power over the masses with tyrant-type punitive damages contrary to most faiths and religious confessions.

Deductively, I've selected different pillars of light on my journey from the island of darkness from which I've escaped, visualized as a tumultuous body of water between it and the perceived island of light, where welcoming shores await. I find myself in uncertainty, and without GPS, I look for buoys of light that will lead me to a destination where I'll recognize the shores I desperately search for. I believe the first buoy of light on this journey so far is love, although I still struggle to define and apply it in agape form. Through the window of my mind, I see that I can no longer depend on religion to direct or define things for me. I have come up, in my mind, with an individualistic definition for myself and the good of my existence in this physical realm. I see this light being defined by my heart's desire for a paradigm shift in a changed perception of agape love collectively, regardless of religious belief. In moving toward the light through the window of my mind, I can now see my new definition of agape love to be enhanced and helpful in the other two forms of love. The new agape belief focuses on the humanities of our civilization and the standardization of equality.

Through the window of my mind, moving toward the light

required that I see myself in everyone. It renewed my perception of "Do unto others as you would have them do unto you." After unbiased examination of myself, I know what I think, I know what I want, I know my self-worth, and I know what I'm deserving of in this realm owned by no one. Toward the light, I now see why I'm glad man doesn't control the sunshine, for he may not have let it shine on me. Moving toward the light, I'm glad man can't order the rain, for he may have refused to water my grain. I found, in examination of myself, thoughts that were no more than shortcomings. There have been times when I believed someone was undeserving or unworthy of the same things I covet or presently have. In new enlightenment of agape love, this is my moment of seeing the concept of deliverance through the window of my mind. I move toward the next buoy of light with the hope of detaching more debilitating thoughts that my God would find unacceptable.

Renewed through the window of my mind and steadfast toward the pillar of light that's guided me through seasons of night and presently across the rift created by my self-mutilating addiction, I again feel my soul exposed to heaven and hell simultaneously as I make my new definition of love my daily practiced belief. Enlightenment along this journey has proven that love contains the secret substance of abundant life, which leads me into being a better person for myself and the overall collective.

In the wilderness of this vast drift over stormy seas full of uncertainty, I visualize buoys of light leading me closer to the shores of deliverance. I've touched the buoy of justification, with a bold inscription of declaration announcing my innocence from the guilt of sin and placing me back into the light of restorative righteousness. I've touched the buoy of regeneration, and it displayed an inscription about the promise of being born again by and through spiritual enlightenment of a second birth. I currently have in sight the buoy of sanctification, and I'm looking at a holographic image fixed atop, indicative of the positioning of my in-between soul. As I remain steadfast in my journey toward the light, warning signals appear with a sea of alternative outcomes. This sophisticated dimmer switch was a tool for my destruction, but I now use it to my advantage for good as I move toward the light, using this dimmer switch to illuminate anything bright. I've reached a buoy with the inscription *Sanctification*, and I just want to stop and hold on. I want to stay in this blessed zone of this light. Holding on to this buoy would be the ultimate find on this journey toward the light. If it were up to me, I'd just stay here and bask in this light of sanctification. I reach out and touch this buoy, tired from the journey toward the light. I read the mind-boggling inscription, and in my peripheral vision, I see, emerging around me, warning signs flashing messages of affirmation: "You've come too far to turn back now. You've reached the point of no need to return. The light gets brighter from here."

I read the inscription: "Here you'll be set apart from your flesh, allowing spiritual vision to recognize your image in the mirror to examine your likeness to the Creator. If flaws appear, you have the supernatural power to correct anything in the realm of sanctification to keep yourself set apart from that flesh that doesn't want to take a backseat."

I now feel a sense of shedding unneeded weight. I feel blinders being removed. I feel as if I'm in an unmasking procedure requiring that I break the seal of my mask first to take a breath of what could be imminent death before others break the seals on their masks.

I reluctantly let go of the buoy of sanctification and return to perpetual motion in moving toward the next saving light. I see in the distance a buoy of what appears to be glorification. Suddenly, it seems as if a current of power puts me on a collision course with this big buoy of glorification. I now feel things added to my belief. I can feel self-actualization. I can feel the practice of giving to others as I would give unto myself, added to "Do unto others as you would do unto yourself."

Enlightenment from the mere touch of this buoy causes an explosion of pathways to uncharted light found only in the supernatural realm. The inscription on this life-keeping buoy representing glorification comes in a familiar voice saying, "This is the beginning of the ultimate state of anyone who believes. After death, we become like our Creator."

Astonished but not deterred, I let go with the futile expectation of death. I feel the salt increasing the buoyancy of my soul, and I feel the power of this water now carrying me into a new light. I recognize that I'm exceedingly glad to be alive. In my gratitude for the journey in my life, I feel like giving glory right now and every day for the rest of my life.

In deliverance through the window of my mind, I start with visualizations of my current position; then I pivot these visualizations into the position longed for. The title of the chapter is "Moving toward the Light," and this has become the holy motivation fuel, igniting the need for change.

It allowed me to look up for the pillar of light by night that's guided me from birth. It is allowing me to hold on to the flickering light of the beginning of this journey of recovery. It allowed me to surrender and lowered my head in humility, gesturing contrition. I'm now basking in gratitude as the light's reflection off the water turns into a pathway to lit shores.

I recognize change. I can feel again, and I can see again, so I must be getting close to the light I've been seeking. Despite the arduous journey and the knowledge gained, I still, in awareness, contemplate religion. I find religion to be interesting and complex but can become perplexed and confused across the spectrums of religions. I now, in my belief in Christianity, have come into divine enlightenment through the window of my mind, wherein I no longer attempt to explain or describe God, nor do I strive to justify with fleshly words the God I serve. I'm on the proving grounds, and I now desire to prove through apperception of my thoughts, words, and deeds. As I look to the future, I know about the important moments I need to be prepared for: births, graduations, marriages, and funerals. I imagine some of the most consequential moments, to which I'd rather have a spiritual response than a fleshly reaction.

I've examined the righteousness shown to me by the God I believe in, and I'm aware and conscious that his ways are far better than my own self-righteousness. The loving-kindness and tender mercies shown toward me have given me a sense of gratefulness that leads me into my deliberate process of forgiveness. In the gratitude and content happiness, I ponder the provisions of mercies that I freely administer toward anyone. These are principles I choose to be empowered for by the grace shown to me by the God I want to imitate.

In deliverance through the window of my mind, moving toward the light, I now consider the fruits of the Spirit while I examine the reflection cast back at me with perfection according to the spiritual understanding recently secured on this journey of recovery in all things considering the flesh.

I went to sleep late with a new and fresh revelation, yet I again awaken to apply the divine part of this new enlightenment in needed moments for my children and their children's children so that I might prove my empirical practicing beliefs to be far better for the sake of my humanity and, more importantly, the nation of my seed's reality of such humanity. I now, in my blessings, embrace these seeds with more frequency with my physical and mental abilities, motivated by the memories of my grandmother's cozy little house. In my grandmother's house, I remember a verbally expressed opinion of God and religion, which gave me a sense of uncertainty, that I now find an appalling statement: "The Bible was written to control or govern humanity."

I've also heard this notion conveyed by a small percentage of people today, but I no longer feel a sense of uncertainty, due to the divine revelation given in my suffering crossing this rift of my self-imposed darkness to a faith-imposed illumination of my future and into a brighter light about God, who I now know to be greater than once believed.

I know the perception of God that was given to me by word of mouth and by the pictures hanging in many churches, which depict their imaginative creation of who God is and what he looks like. I've listened to some of the greatest sermons, and I've read the Word extensively. It wasn't until I reached fifty-eight years of living that I, in this book titled *Deliverance through the Window of My Mind*, began to realize that I still can't come up with a personal description of God, but I believe God to be greater than the perception given in the inspired written words in the Bible.

I can't speak for you, but I've often worshipped, prayed to, and praised the image of a man with physical attributes of humans. The Word says, "Let us make man in our image," and I've believed that in a physical and literal sense in the past more than the spiritual. I now focus on the spiritual aspect of the likeness in his image, for I now find it inextricable in the transformation and renewing of my mind by the Holy Spirit.

I am being sentient and aware of my mind, spirit, and soul without description of such. I've come to the realization that if I was made in his image, I too am greater than I believe. I can't describe the mind, spirit, and soul I'm conscious of in this physical realm of my reality, so I no longer feel it necessary to try to describe the physical realities of God. I now feel the supernatural essence and attributes of God to feel and familiarize myself with his spiritual presence, which I've experienced in this physical realm of existence. The love of family was the initial unction in my desire to be released from any stronghold on my life, but it evolved into a sense of gratitude that pervasively turned my desire into not grieving the Holy Spirit, which I cannot see but can feel.

I now beg the questions "Are the attributes of love, compassion, grace, mercy, and forgiveness described in the Bible not good?" and "Am I greater than I believe?"

Yes, for me, these attributes are far better than once believed, and by using these attributes, I've empirically shown the positive results of such attributes. When followed, they create a far better self, a better atmosphere by proximity, and a better world atmosphere for the existence of mankind. I, in an elevated awakening, truly believing that I too am greater, can now esteem all others to be the same. This is where we humans perpetuate the worst attributes of supposed selflessness, which lack empathy and promote ungodly principles, as we continue confessing with our mouths religious beliefs while dressed in fleshly deceit to deny others the same things we believe we deserve.

This was a great part of my titling this chapter "Moving toward the Light." This journey has opened my eyes to more than deliverance from addiction, for my addiction was no more than a symptom of the arduous journey of my life infused with fragments of pain, hints of heartbreak, and sprinkles of trauma amid continuous uncertainty. I allowed myself to succumb to a substance that was rendering me and the future of seeds into further dysfunction. This led me to the title of this book: *Deliverance through the Window of My Mind*. This is not to say that I'm all I need to recover myself from this self-imposed self-imprisonment of darkness that held me captive through cell bars that weren't even locked. The answer was in the epiphany that God is greater than I could imagine and that my being made in God's image makes me also greater than I believe.

I've tried man's help in recovery, and I suggest you try one of the many forms of help extended to relieve people of suffering from the disease of addiction. I see the light in the maintenance by AA, NA, CA, and Celebrate Recovery. I even have respect in Smart Recovery, and with the expansion of Al-Anon, we can now attempt to bring families into the process of recovery. It's incumbent for me to use all the tools given by man, but it's imperative for me to use the tool of the Spirit provisioned with purpose, PWP, and the weapons of faith and hope.

The power invested in me by God, within the power of my mind, is invaluable for the exodus journey of deliverance from this debilitating disease.

In the next chapter, I will give scriptures and other methods of belief that have given me enlightenment. The scriptures I've read and heard over the years continue to give provision to fresh perspective and elevated thought processes. I now look to apply these scriptures with incessant, minute mindfulness. The intent for these scriptures is a renewed mindset desperately needed for my deliverance.

I invite you to become participatory in your state of bondage, whether your vice is drug or alcohol addiction; unnatural sex affection; hatred; unforgiveness; gossip; anger; or anything else by thought, word, or deed that is nonproductive and contrary to the essence of the Creator of love, grace, and mercy. I don't tell people what they should do, nor do I have a mathematical equation for overall deliverance. What I look for is elevated thought through the evidence of my desire to become a better person. I now use the empirical evidence of the spirit or essence of such beliefs to prove my being a far better way in this physical existence I'm blessed to be part of, despite its hellacious moments.

In my conscious state of being, evidence of my subconscious in the process of healing is recognized. I feel I've reached the distant shore where raindrops of hope fall, where the sunshine's radiance covers 360 degrees of certainty, and where the blue skies of peace prevail. I now am fresh out of this addiction and faced with the painful waters of shame, guilt, and embarrassment. I swim through waves of repercussions, awaiting the change in my mind. With each stroke toward the light of this island, I shift and shed the conscious thoughts in my mind and examine my ability to be truly honest with myself to expose the hidden agendas of my flesh. Here my sincere contrition leads me into levels of desperate change. In the strokes that move me closer to the light, I use scripture as pathway buoy markers, detecting changes. Not long ago, I stood on the opposite shore with my addiction, hopeless, while gazing upon the distant shore across the raging sea between. I made it with all the bits and pieces that remain, consciously competent of all I've gained and must gain.

SEVEN

OPERATING IN REPOSITIONED LIGHT

I n order to recognize myself as being repositioned, I had to recognize myself as being out of position. One's concept of position differs depending on the environment one is raised in. One's perspective of position is a culmination of experiences of the past and one's hope of an apperceived future position designed by the hope of what could be. Meanwhile, I continue to search for a sense of peace and certainty that can only be derived from contrasting those good yet pointed frames of reference given to me in times past. In deliverance through the window of my mind, I began my point of reference with examples of elders who accepted their assignment to be used in the breaking of generational curses with strongholds that had tentacles touching a variety of mindsets at one time found to be acceptable. The words were sometimes hurtful in the correction, but I believe they were said in an effort to deter self-destruction and cut the vines perpetuating these curses with the sharpest tool available (i.e., verbal assault). These consistent reminders were given by any means necessary in love.

Now I recognize those subliminal messages delivered without words to be the most profitable for my well-being. I see now a blueprint within the framework to go beyond to reach self-actualization. If that wasn't possible for me, depending on my choices, I could count on at least attaining a semblance of success. These subliminal messages imparted the tying up of one's bootstraps daily to face the world again on another day, regardless of its lack of light. These subliminal messages made me believe that despite the dysfunctions in the family, even if you have to feed them until they look like you dysfunctions. The subliminal messages in reference to the kids were most important. These messages imparted into my subconscious the need to operate in the light of what's right within the three forms of love. These messages created a heart of empathy for those less fortunate than I am (e.g., if you don't want your kids to go without, know that no one else does either). We all know that the suggestion of *without* goes further than physiological needs of water and food to include health care, education, housing, and the assurance of society moving forward in its attempt to perfect the imperfect existence of mankind.

In the previous chapter, "Moving toward the Light," I mentioned that particular scriptures helped in the navigation of my repositioning in the light. I also mentioned the buoys of belief (i.e., justification, regeneration, sanctification, and glorification), for they gave me the strength to endure. I use these doctrines in a pyramid form. I use these doctrines of belief to examine my position within the parameters or boundaries of operating in the repositioned light I now find myself in. The revelation of scriptures is consistent in the renewing of my mind, and continual enlightenment through discussion with others, at their understanding, is priceless. The following list will give indication of the proven power of spiritual kinetics in small-group discussion.

Scripture to examine and think about in our addictions:

Philippians 1:1–6
Philippians 3:12–13
Philippians 4:8–9
Philippians 4:12–13
Hebrews chapter 11
Romans 1:28–32
Romans 10:1–4
1 Corinthians 2:9
1 Corinthians 9:24–27

Discuss these in your mind and in small-group recovery meetings over time.

These are things to compare and measure my spiritual competency in light of justification, regeneration, sanctification, and glorification. These scriptures can be interchangeable, and scriptures can also be added through personal enlightenment.

The following scriptures are a list I used in changing my mindset and are an integral portion of regaining my conscious competency in regard to my repositioning in the light I'm now operating in:

Romans 6:1–7
Romans 8:1–39
Romans 10:17
Romans 13:11–14
1 Corinthians 1:26–29
1 Corinthians 2:9
1 Corinthians 10:12–14
Galatians 5:1

James 1:12–16

Romans 12:1–2

Romans 7:14–25

1 Corinthians 15:58

2 Corinthians 4:8–18

2 Corinthians 12:7–10

Galatians 5:16–24

Ephesians 3:14–20

Ephesians 5:8–21

Ephesians 6:10–20

Philippians 1:1–6

Philippians 4:8–9

Philippians 3:12–14

Colossians 1:9–12

Colossians 2:6–10

Colossians 3:1–17

Colossians 4:5–6

1 Thessalonians 5:18–28

1 Timothy 4:14–16

2 Timothy 2:22–26

James 2:14–19

2 Peter 1:1–11

I keep close to my heart another theory I learned in college as a young man that led me into yearning for the manifestation of it for myself. Awakened in my deliverance from a form of darkness in my addiction, I had to come back into a deeper understanding of examining my thoughts, words, and deeds to compare my positioning according to my understanding of each level of Maslow's hierarchy of needs. It is the most eye-opening or get-woke form of philosophy for me. This pyramid models the building of a society in which just about everyone can reach self-actualization deservedly by the design of the Creator of our existence.

Interaction is solicited by your studying of this theory to come up with your own interpretation for application according to your evolving understanding. It will give a different perspective of a new conception of worldliness, in which the entire collective and everyone's interests are the central focus, instead of the type of greed that excludes the needs of a percentage of the collective. Meanwhile, in a populating world where natural and intentional tragedies (e.g., mental health problems, mass shootings, drug and alcohol addictions, and many other stumbling blocks) continue adding to the dysfunctions being encountered in our existence, a course correction is needed because continuing practices of old are contributing to a new generation of unteachable children, whom we are desperately depending on to be good stewards of the future.

In my deliverance through the window of my mind, I came to the conclusion by the art of reasonable deduction that these dysfunctions are direct results derived from the prevalent environments still causing and allowing systemic racism and systemic inequality to sit at the collective table of life. Wake up, and pay attention to the wickedness that has an ulterior motive to create a society of haves and have-nots.

In order for me to operate in the light of this darkness, I must hold tight to the newly established virtues of love, empathy for others, and decency toward others to be the model of my belief. This is deliverance through the window of my mind. I've exchanged my addiction and imperfections for a renewed mindset driven by love.

I said to myself, "Use these scriptures for application for yourself. Use these scriptures for discussion in small-group settings. They are for your mental application over time to attain a renewed mindset for yourself." I also use the theory of Maslow's hierarchy of needs for that self I refer to often, and I use empirical proof of experiences with God or the Creator or higher power that self in me believes and has faith in. This is the formula. This is the procedure. These are the practices and methods I apply to that self, who is actually no joke or third person. It's me. In deliverance through the window of my mind, these are the tools essential for me, because they represent my faith in, and acknowledgment of, something greater than myself, which I trust and depend upon to ease the pain from this wicked and perverse world.

As I operate in the repositioned light, it's important to decipher wrong from right. In my higher level of consciousness, my mind intentionally looks at the beforehand intellectuals giving credence to truths and facts. We can all develop a process for identifying truth, and I use the following narrative to show that a heightened state of mind can lead you to look to be part of a solution for the collective. I'll use the "Just say no" campaign pertaining to drugs, which was created and pushed by the first lady back in the early 1980s, because it has a backdrop that was not seen until sometime afterward. This program took on a life of its own, and it was with good intent yet not justified in truth. Years later, we found out through investigative reporting that the US government, in high places, was involved in a sophisticated laundering scheme for weapons that included the sale and distribution of crack cocaine to inner cities across the nation. This is just one devastating truth found after examination of the backdrop of the matter. This particular atrocity resulted in the destruction of millions of families and still has a devastating impact on life among us today. This particular atrocity has created a valley of dry bones that is being added to daily. Victims yet to come soon will be skulls found inches below the eroding earth, indicative of preeminent death planned by man. A myriad of such atrocities are committed by mankind. I only go back to the immediate things that affect me. That is not to say that the slavery imposed years ago doesn't have an effect on me today, because I know it does, but it can no longer impede my hope, despite its residue. In elevated thought, it's my responsibility to search for the truth of any manner before I wave a flag. I do not agree to fly any banner until it's passed these scanners.

In deliverance through the window of my mind, a risen thought pattern has changed my mindset about any addictive stronghold, whether it be of a substance, spiritual iniquities, hatred in any form, turning a blind eye to atrocities, excessive greed, dishonesty, selfishness, piety, or sexual indiscretions. All these things have self-destructive tendencies with fallout to overflow onto the less fortunate and the loved ones in our world.

The heightened thought pattern delivered a gift of transparency within me that provokes an easily accessible truth. This elevated thought pattern increased my discernment of the intentions of myself and others, despite eloquent rhetoric that could be full of defecation, with repeated sound bites that capture those with a limited continuousness or those I identify as having small minds, who are willing to continue pissing on me and telling me that it's raining.

Operating in the light demands evidence of works in you, me, and the world that are reflective of the work of the sun for our existence here on earth. Operating in the light becomes like the work of the rain in our existence, in tandem with that of the marvelous sun. Operating in the light is a spiritual virtual reality to see those we can trust to be stewards of the sun and rain because they have no ulterior motives for such power and have no preconceived condition for the distribution of something that is freely given by our Creator without conditions. I live my life now with this thought process in mind, and I pray that collectively, as a species, we will see in the Spirit the need for change. If this is wokeism, don't wake me up! This is how I plan to operate. This is my religion. This is how I was delivered through the window of my mind.

EIGHT

LIVING IN THE LIGHT

woke up one morning and had a blank check in hand to fill in any amount I wanted to receive. I couldn't come up with a number. I took the opportunity while pondering the perfect number. I concluded that I had to first do some work that was proven to align itself with the empirical truths of my heart's desire. The most immediate and most important aspects of living in the light are in the rewards from continuously doing the next right thing. I am reminded of many sleepless nights and the negative consequences and results imposed by my small-mindedness. I remember the pain of longing for the important things to manifest.

Considering my heart's desires, I've been trying to articulate what it can't say and to explain what you can't see. I put into my mind some of the most precious memories I hold on to dearly from 4115 South Benton, 1143 Oakland, 709 Georgia, 3700 Topping, and right across the wood line in River Park, where my cousin Sherita stayed. In those spaces and places, I truly cared about the well-being of all the characters encountered, whether they were blood or friend. In the small pathways of 1143 Oakland, I learned and witnessed goodness and love. At 3700 Topping, I was taught how to practice goodness and love. At 4115 South Benton, I actualized the concept of these experiences with my immediate family, whom I've eaten with for years, with whom I've slept under the same roof for years, and with whom I've cried and laughed for a lifetime.

Living in the light has increased my articulation of my heart's desires, and I can now explain and describe what should be seen. This is what I see living in the light.

I woke up at my son's house right outside Seattle, Washington. I could see shadows reflecting from beneath the door in the room I was sleeping in. I could faintly hear voices attempting to avoid detection with the greatest respect. I smiled as I got out of the bed, went straight to the door, slowly put my hand on the knob, and opened the door. Sitting in crisscross position were all three of my grandchildren. The looks in their eyes spoke volumes without utterance. That visitation was short but impactful. I saw them ride their bicycles to Puget Sound as my son, his wife, and I walked behind. I took pictures of them and the beautiful earth scenery to have evidence of that dreamlike moment. In the backyard, the little boy in me kicked in when I saw the kids jumping on a trampoline, and I decided to join in. It was a memorable moment as I lay face up, looking at the sunny blue sky, while listening to the joy of my grandchildren.

Only a few days later, I was in Kansas City, where I spent the night at another son's house, where the pattern repeated itself with a slight variance. That trip had an additional permanent fixture to the family, which caused me to sleep on the bottom of a bunk bed in a room with a grandson. Early the next morning, I saw the sunlight as it began to illuminate my emotions. I looked around, and my grandson was sitting in his chair.

He asked, "Are you getting up now, Pawpaw?"

I said yes and, in return, got a morning itinerary that seemed well planned. I surrendered with great joy and great anticipation of the first birthday party in my life, my sixtieth, which was planned for that evening. I enjoyed being present in the moment. I was trying to sneak up on my newborn granddaughter, whom my son was guarding due to the COVID epidemic. I learned to look down the road to hold her at another time, for I knew that COVID stuff too would pass!

The party was beautiful in its aesthetics and even more beautiful in the people who came to celebrate it with me. My oldest niece drove my oldest brother and oldest sister from Minneapolis, and my two brothers and their wives from Kansas City came also. The twins were responsible for their daddy's first birthday party with a Lakers theme. I asked them to invite two of my friends I considered to be a great part of my life, and they showed up. These two are part of that little boy in myself whom I've been looking to recapture, and our time spent was priceless. Three of my first wife's sisters were there with the same love for me as always. I had seven of my grandchildren there and some friends from my kids' acquaintances. It was awesome, and my heart was glad! I left that party and joined another party with some of my schoolmates I hadn't seen in some time, and it too was wonderful.

Almost a year later, I was invited to the twins' birthday party, and it was spectacular. I finally got a chance to hold my now one-year-old granddaughter without the fear of COVID.

The night before I was to fly back to California, I decided to stay in a hotel room with my daughter, her husband, and three of my grandchildren, along with her sisters' two kids—a total of eight people in a small, cozy room. In the room, I lay behind a pull curtain that divided the room. I could hear my daughter tell the kids to be quiet because Pawpaw was trying to get some sleep. I listened to the individuals and found out something about all of them. It seemed the youngest didn't care or didn't understand, because he kept running back and forth without regard for my presence. I could feel tension in their attempts to quiet him down, so I pulled the curtain back and made myself part of the room. I let them know they were not bothering me, and I decided it was an opportunity to familiarize myself even more with the seeds created by my seed. The little boy in me showed up and began chasing a one-year-old grandson, who had a great deal of joy and happiness when I let him think he was getting away. We were all laughing, and our hearts were full of joy. I jumped on the extra bed and asked my two oldest granddaughters to take a picture with me. Afterward, I asked my two oldest grandsons to jump on the bed and take a picture. I sensed some reluctance, I mentioned it, and we all began to laugh again. I've been invited to family events and gathered memories to motivate the unexplainable illumination of love, which has more value than money.

I look at the blank check again, and the amount doesn't matter, for I've found relationships with my offspring to be the unmeasurable treasure at the end of the day. I can now articulate the desires of my heart, and I can explain what my heart wants to see by the experiences I've described since my repositioning. My renewed subconscious, which is proven by the conscious state of my existence, now resembles spoken love manifested. This love is now in my DNA, and it's a part of me, due to the spiritual understanding on my journey to recovery from most, if not all, strongholds that impede my ability to love. It is reflective of the empirical love shown to me from above, and it has proven itself in the actions of the past, with the deliberate intent of doing the same in the future.

In deliverance through the window of my mind, I've found I have plenty of opportunities to enhance the narrative of my life, the narrative of my legacy, and the narrative to be spoken over me when the physical portion of my life is over. I am deliberate in my mindfulness, my meditation, and my self-correction, which can only be found in and by honest self-evaluation. This contrition leads me into sincere repentance. It is the stabilizing force to maintain the repositioning of my life with light.

In deliverance through the window of my mind, I look at what I see, and I visualize what I'd like to see. Even if it doesn't turn out exactly as I saw it, I'm satisfied with a close resemblance to anything that is good and comes from above.

There is a great motivational speaker by the name of Les Brown, who said, "I'd rather be prepared for an opportunity and not have one than have an opportunity and not be prepared." In deliverance through the window of my mind, I'd rather be prepared to look into the eyes of my grandchildren and answer the most important question that will be asked, derived from the windows of their minds. I'd rather be prepared to exude love and goodness into the windows, or eyes, of everyone I encounter. I'd rather be prepared to turn the other cheek to prove power under control. I'd rather be prepared to receive all the promises and provisions of God. I'd rather be prepared for the opportunity to go to heaven and have it not be real than have an opportunity to go to heaven and not be prepared. If the prerequisites for heaven or eternal life are being connected to the fruits of the Spirit and confession of faith in propitiation, then I choose a path of goodness, for it makes a better world for all. I'd rather wake up dead and then realize the promises of God and know with conviction the preparedness purposely planned for such an opportunity.

If you're struggling, know that you're more than capable of overcoming any obstacle attempting to hinder your journey to self-actualization with God on your side. Love is the cure to all spiritual ailments known to mankind. Wake up, and find love!

Until the next book, stay blessed, my friends!

BRIAN'S CORNER

I awake daily with an overwhelming sense of gratitude, sentient, while tear tracks of times past, present, and future appear. I'm reminded in spirit of the mindfulness necessary to love and of my new spiritual truth imputed to impartiality to examine myself without prejudice and, with spiritual sensibility, avoid reproach. I go through my day with immense hope of finding someone in need of being seen or given hope. I then beseech the Lord for the prayer to pray, the words to say, the thought to think, and the song to sing for those souls who are found in the alleys of life. I go into the evening with deliberate confessions of my thoughts, words, and deeds unacceptable to God. I go into my night with contrition as I ask God for forgiveness and mercy, knowing his promise to restore my righteousness as he creatively renews my self-being, giving me the ability to continuously metamorphose into increased love. I go into my sleep having prayed and resting in his grace, only to awaken with the opportunity and strength to do it again in the light of deliverance through the window of my mind.

FRANK BUFFA'S CORNER

My name is Frank Buffa. I've been working in the field of addiction for 17 years, the last 13 years with Hope By The Sea. I also have a private practice. I've been teaching Emotional Released through writing. The goal being finding your peace of mind. How do you find peace of mind?

You remove everything that in your perception is bothering it. I teach clients to express the way they think and more importantly the way they feel in writing. It's a metaphysic approach or what I call Bio-Meta-Physical. Meta meaning beyond, so how what is beyond physical affects our Bio or life. What is beyond physical? Thoughts and feelings. Mental health starts with peace of mind. That's the reason that it is important to be aware and pay attention to our thinking and feeling processes. I started on this path because of personal issues. I had bad depression and anxiety for part of my life. Very crippling. I wanted to find a way to get better ad that was the beginning of the journey.

My group is called The Work. I chose this name because of realizing that it takes efforts if you want to change. In my group we pay attention to what is bothering us right now. We realign the subconscious and the conscious so they can collaborate instead of working against each other. We deal with all the negative from our past, all our traumas that need to be let go of to find peace. Memories can't be deleted but we can release the emotions that they are carrying and find peace of mind.

Printed in the United States
by Baker & Taylor Publisher Services